COUNTER INSURGENCY IN NIGERIA AND THE LAKE CHAD OPTION

NNAMDI CHRISTIANTUS EKWOM

Defence Adviser Nigerian High Commission Yaoundé

COUNTER INSURGENCY IN NIGERIA AND THE LAKE CHAD OPTION

iUniverse books may be ordered through booksellers or by contacting:

iUniverse
1663 Liberty Drive
Bloomington, IN 47403
www.iuniverse.com
844-349-9409

Because of the dynamic nature of the Internet, any web addresses or links contained in this book may have changed since publication and may no longer be valid. The views expressed in this work are solely those of the author and do not necessarily reflect the views of the publisher, and the publisher hereby disclaims any responsibility for them.

Any people depicted in stock imagery provided by Getty Images are models, and such images are being used for illustrative purposes only. Certain stock imagery © Getty Images.

ISBN: 978-1-6632-3131-4 (sc)
ISBN: 978-1-6632-3132-1 (e)

Print information available on the last page.

iUniverse rev. date: 12/13/2021

ABSTRACT

Insurgency is essentially a form of uprising or rebellion against a government authority with the aim of deposing such a government or rendering it incapable of carrying out her basic functions. Injustice, divisions and all forms of cleavages that exist in our societies are the major breeders of insurgency. Counterinsurgency is therefore a whole gamut of actions of the government to counter insurgency. Though counter insurgency in Nigeria dates back to the pre independent era, this paper is focused mainly on the post independent (1960 – 2020) counter insurgencies with peculiarity to the activities of the Boko Haram terrorist group. The Movement for the Emancipation of Niger Delta, the Biafra War and the Boko Haram terrorist desire to establish a caliphate within the African sub region are some of the insurrectional activities that characterized the Nigerian Counter Insurgency operations since independence. The Boko Haram terrorist group that was founded 19 years ago by late Mohammed Yusuf has continued to unleash terror on the people of North Eastern Nigeria. These activities are predominant in the states of Borno, Yobe and Adamawa. This group has also made a lot of incursions into Cameroon, Chad and Niger Republic in a bid to establish an Islamic state in the region.

They are reported to have killed over 30,000 civilians within the last 10 years. The government of Nigeria has embarked on a series of reforms and restructure of the armed forces to meet the challenges of the Boko Haram terrorists. Capacity building was central in the efforts of the government to close the gaps observed in the skills of the officers and soldiers in carrying out their responsibilities. Consequently, a number of special forces training schools were established. Through the instrumentality of the Multinational Joint Task Forces and the creation of Forward Operating Bases and Super Camps, the armed forces of the Federal Republic of Nigeria has been able to degrade the activities of this group considerably. However, revitalization of livelihood options especially for youth in the Lake Chad region remain crucial to durable peace, development and stability in the entire region.

INTRODUCTION

The Oxford Advance Learners' Dictionary defines an insurgent as a person fighting against government forces in her or his own country[1]. However other terms like rebellion, insurrection and uprising are also correctly used in describing insurgency. Insurgency therefore is an uprising or rebellion against a government authority with the aim of deposing such a government. This is usually as a result of a discontent with the policies and programs of the government, therefore the insurgents generally strive to gain freedom through staging rebellious activities that could weaken the structure and probably bring down the existing government. Note that in international law, insurgents are not belligerents as they are not recognized by other nations or the United Nations[2]. Smaller insurgents without popular support that is easily crushed by constituted authority are most times referred to as brigands, criminals or bandits. Insurgency and terrorism are closely related and sometimes inseparable as is clearly evident in the activities of Boko Haram Terrorist (BHT) in the north eastern part of

---

[1] Oxford Advance Learners Dictionary.
[2] Gupta, Rashi, Recognition of Insurgent and Belligerent Organisations in International Law (April 23, 2014).

Nigeria. Not all insurgents apply violence in pursuant of their objectives as against a terrorist whose primary object is to use violence to create terror and fear in the minds of innocent citizens in furtherance of their objective.

In view of the foregoing, Counter Insurgency (COIN) operation involves a whole gamut of activities, including military, paramilitary, political, economic, psychological and civic actions organized by a government to neutralize the insurgents. For effective COIN operations, it must be clearly understood that insurgency thrives on social cleavages such as ethnic, language, political, economic and other forms of social imbalances. These are divisions that have characterized our world today, particularly the African continents. Hence, the prevalence of insurgency in virtually all counties in Africa which Nigeria is not an exception. The purpose of this paper therefore is to examine various efforts of Nigeria in fighting insurgency with a view to drawing lessons and providing a standard for determining the success or failure of a COIN operation. It is expected to contribute in improving the conduct of COIN operations in Nigeria, Africa or elsewhere in the world. It further considers the option of recharging lake chad as a critical soft counterinsurgency measure. Though the history of insurgency in Nigeria dates back to the pre - independent days, this paper will focus on post –independence COIN operation with particular emphasis on the Counter insurgency operations against the BHT in Nigeria. This work will look at the History of Insurgency in Nigeria, Activities of BHT in Nigeria, and Government Actions against the BHT group, finally there will be an appraisal of government actions to determine success or failure. Finally the lake chad option as a soft approach for COIN will be examined.

METHODOLOGY

Primary and secondary sources were used in the course of this work. The primary sources are essentially from personal interaction with front line officers in the ongoing COIN operations against the Boko Haram terrorist group including some members of the Multi National Joint Task Force (MNJTF) in the northeast. The central role the author plays as the Defense Adviser particularly with information management between the Nigerian military and the Cameroonian military in the fight against insurgents provided the opportunity for personal and telephone interactions with key stake holders in the COIN operations against the BHT. The author had the opportunity to interact personally with the current Commander of the Multinational Joint Task Force (MNJTF) Major General AK Ibrahim and it was very insightful. The secondary sources are mainly from the internet and other electronic and print publications on the subject matter.

STATEMENT OF THE PROBLEM

The armed forces of Nigeria have been engaged in numerous COIN operations from the days of the Nigerian civil war in 1967 to date. Some of these engagements include the civil war in Liberia and Sierra Leone, militancy in the Niger delta, Biafra agitations and the BHT. Though most of these challenges have been conclusively dealt with by the armed forces of Nigeria, the lingering activities of the BHT on the Nigeria territory has continued to generate debates on the government's claim to have technically defeated this group. This has in many ways impacted negatively on the morale of the troops in the frontline and the massive support expected form the civil population particularly from the high political leadership. Hence the call for the change of Service Chiefs, despite the change of the Service Chiefs in January 2021, the problem still persists hence the look at the effect of the disappearance of lake chad on the security of the region. This is a problem this paper seeks to address by providing a yard stick to measure the success of counter insurgency operations bearing in mind that situations of insurgency globally may not necessarily be identical. The paper further considers the option of recharging lake chad as a panacea for insecurity in the region.

HISTORY OF INSURGENCY IN NIGERIA

Though the history of insurgency in Nigeria predates the independence era, this is primarily as a result of the activities that surrounded the struggle for the country's independence. In the Nigerian post-independent period, notable insurgency are as discussed subsequently.

Niger Delta Volunteer Force. Though the history of insurgency in Nigeria predates the independence era. This is primarily as a result of the activities that surrounded the struggle for the country's independence. The first organized post independent attempt to insurgency in Nigeria may be traced to the movement for the liberation of the Niger Delta (MLND) led by Major Isaac Jasper Adaka Boro.[3] The group was agitating against the continued exploitation of oil and gas resources in the region which caused a monumental environmental degradation that adversely affected the wellbeing of the citizens of this region as it deprived them access to their only source of livelihood. Consequently, Major Isaac Adaka Boro, an Ijaw nationalist formed the Niger

---

[3] Allswell Osini Muzan, Insurgency in Nigeria: Addressing the causes as part of the solution

Delta Volunteer Force(NDVF), this group declared the Niger Delta Republic on 23 Feb 1966.[4] However, this group was quickly crushed by the Armed Forces of the Federal Republic of Nigeria within 12 days of its existence. Nonetheless, this was eventually the foundation upon which The Movement for the Emancipation of the Niger Delta (MEND) was built. MEND was a more violent arm of the struggle of the Niger Delta people. It was a coalition of various armed groups including cult groups who were aggrieved by the activities of international oil companies in the Niger Delta. They launched a series of attacks on oil installations following a mutual agreement[5]. This eventually led to the reduction of daily crude oil production in Nigeria to about 75%.[6] The government launched a series of coordinated attacks that largely degraded the capacity of this group; this was followed by a series of negotiations with the leadership of the group that culminated into an amnesty granted by president Yar'Adua on 25 July 2009.

The Nigerian Civil War. The post independent political environment in Nigeria was characterized with numerous social cleavages coupled with the tensions created by political differences and economic divisions at that time. This eventually led to a coup d'état of 15 January 1966 which was alleged to be ethnically motivated as it eliminated the prominent leaders from

---

[4] Kubiat Umana, History and Causes of 8 Insurgencies in Nigeria, August 3, 2018

[5] KIMIEBI, IMOMOTIMI EBIENFA (2010). *OIL, MILITANCY AND POLITICAL OPPORTUNITIES IN THE NIGER DELTA.* ISBN 978-3848483907.

[6] Conor Gaffey, Nigeria no Longer Africa's Top Oil Producer, As Militants Cut Production, Newsweek 17 June 2016.

the northern part of the country including Alhaji Tafawa Balewa, the then Prime Minister of Nigeria and Alhaji Ahmadu Bello, the Premier of Northern Nigeria.

It was then followed by a counter coup of 29 July 1966 which was allegedly staged to address the imbalance of the previous Coup d'état. This eventually resulted into ethnic killings and counter killing, hence on 27 May 1967, Colonel Odumegwu Ojukwu declared an independent state which he called the Republic of Biafra. The Federal government of Nigeria deployed forces in the region to quell this Republic and it eventually resulted in a civil war. This war lasted from 1967 to 1970 when the Biafra troops surrendered before the Nigeria Armed Forces. This civil war was probably the most devastating that the continent of Africa has experienced as it was reported to have caused the death of over 3 million people.[7] However, the declaration of Republic of Biafra formed the foundation upon which the Movement for the Actualization of the Sovereign State of Biafra (MASSOB) was created which eventually transformed to what is known today as the Indigenous People of Biafra(IPOB).

Movement for the Actualization of the Sovereign States of Biafra. In 1999, nearly 2 decades after Nigeria civil war, MASSOM was formed by an India trained Lawyer, Ralph Uwazwuike.

This group's objective was not different from those of Colonel Odumegwu Ojukwu who declared the Republic of Biafra in 1967. The group claimed to be non - violent but they adopted the Biafra flag, produced and circulated Biafra currency as a legal

---

[7] S Olawale, Causes of Civil War In Nigeria and its Effects January 3, 2019.

tender in the south eastern part of Nigeria. It also produced and issued passports to the citizen of Biafra who are mostly from the south eastern part of Nigeria. The Federal government found the group responsible for certain violence attack against the police and member of the Armed Force. Consequently, Mr Ralph Uwazulike was arrested in 2005 and was eventually released in 2007. However, as time went on, there was a misunderstanding among the leadership of MASSOB which led to the formation of IPOB by Mr Nnamdi Kanu in 2012.

Indigenous People of Biafra. The activities of IPOB remains a substantial threat to the cooperate existence of the Federal Republic of Nigeria. On 18 September 2017, a Federal High Court in Abuja labelled IPOB a terrorist organization. The leader Nnamdi Kanu was arrested and charged to court on 25 April 2017. He was granted bail on account of ill health, however, he escaped from the country in September 2017 after an encounter with members of the Armed Forces in his residence. However, he was rearrested in June 2021 while on trip to Kenya and brought back to Nigeria to face trials. This group promised to attack prominent Nigerian politicians particularly those from the south eastern part of the country whenever they are seen outside the country. They claimed responsibility for the attack on the former Deputy Senate President, Senator Ike Ekweremadu in Nuremberg Germany in August 2019. Also, they attempted an attack on the Minister of Transport Mr Rotimi Amaechi during an official engagement in Spain in December 2019.

Since the re-arrest of Nnamdi Kanu, this group has stepped up the tempo of their activities, particularly in the South East, where they have killed a number policemen and solders on duty. They have also imposed Monday lockdown on all commercial activities in the South East of Nigeria.

Movement for the Emancipation of Niger Delta. It is pertinent to note that 30 years after the death of Isaac Boro, another Movement for the Emancipation of Niger Delta (MEND) staged a comeback. Following the activities of this group, most of the Niger Delta region was engulfed in conflict. Militant groups from the Ijaw, Itshekiri and Urhobo ethnic groups emerged and most times clashed against each other in fierce battles over the control of oil producing areas within the region. However, by early 2000, these militants group launched attacks on all symbols of government located in the region. International oil companies were not left out in these attacks as many oil platforms were blown up with dynamites causing monumental loss of life and properties with an attendant environmental degradation on account of oil spillage. By 2004, the entire Niger Delta region was heavily militarized by the activities of the insurgents, kidnapping, hostage taking and piracy was rampart within the water ways. Daily oil production in Nigeria, dropped by 75%.[8]

In February 2009, the Nigeria government launched a massive military operation, to flush out the militants. Members of operation Delta Safe patrolled the creeks hunting for the insurgents. All civilian boats within the water ways were stopped and searched for weapons. Numerous camps belonging to the insurgents were raided and destroyed. On 26 Jun 2009, the Federal Government of

---

[8] Conor Gaffey, Nigeria no Longer Africa's Top Oil Producer, As Militants Cut Production, Newsweek 17 June 2016.

Nigeria under President Umar Musa Yar'Adua announced that it would grant amnesty and unconditional pardon to the insurgents who will surrender and drop their weapons. This amnesty was to last for 60 days starting from 6 Aug 2009 and ending on 4 Oct 2009. This presidential amnesty programme was very effective as over 30,000 militant youth dropped their weapons and enrolled into the programme. The security in the Niger Delta has since returned to a near normal situation. Oil production has risen from about 700,000 barrels per day to about 2.4 million barrels per day. This situation aptly demonstrates the effectiveness of a systematic application of non kinetic means in counter insurgency operations. It is pertinent to note that the aggressive military action before the offer of amnesty was highly instrumental to the success of the amnesty programme.

Oodua Peoples Congress. Nigeria also witnessed the formation of the Oodua Peoples Congress (OPC) by the Yoruba ethnic group led by Dr Fredrick Fasehun and Are Gani Adam. This was largely as a result of discontent in the south west region of Nigeria following the annulment of 12 June 1993 presidential election and the death of Chief Moshood Abiola, a prominent businessman and philanthropist from the Yourba ethnic group. He was widely accepted to be the winner of the 12 June 1993 presidential election. This annulment of this election created serious political instability in Nigeria which eventually culminated into the resignation of General Badamosi Babangida, the then head of state and Commander in Chief of the armed forces of Nigeria. General Babangida accepted the responsibility for the annulment of this election but has not given any substantial reason for the cancelation of an election that was perceived to be free and fair by the majority of Nigeria and the international community.

Infuriated by this development, the OPC launched series of attacks in 1993 against some symbols of governance particularly in Lagos State in expression of their discontent. They sometimes expressed the ambition to secede from Nigeria and form a sovereign Oduduwa Republic. Though this group has remained relatively peaceful over time, the government continues to keep an eye over their activities.

The Boko Haram Terrorist Group. The history of Boko Haram insurgency in northern Nigeria can be traced back to a man called Mohammed Maroua born in 1927. He was a renown preacher in Kano state who migrated from Cameroon to Nigeria in 1945.[9] His sermons were usually extreme and strongly against western culture. He was so radical in his religious views that it earned him the name Maitatsine (the one who damns). For him, reading any other book other than the Quran was a sin and a sign of paganism. By 1980, the radicalism and anti-government sermons of Maitatsine caused the Federal Government of Nigeria to go after the group. Consequently, in 1982 the group organized a wide spread riot in Kano State and the subsequent military action resulted in the death of over 4,000 people including Maitatsine himself.

Despite the death of Maitatsine in 1982, his ideology remained a credible threat to the peaceful coexistence of religious groups in the northern part of Nigeria. Some of the followers of

---

[9] Aanu Adegun, MAITATSINE: Story of Nigeria's bloody religious terror of the 80s – Grandmother of Boko Haram (Part 1), Legit 2017

Maitatsine continued to propagate his ideology and even nursed the desire to turn Nigeria into an Islamic state. Consequently, in 2002, Twenty years after the death of Maitatsine, Boko Haram was formed by Mohammed Yusuf, a fundamentalist who was influenced by the message of Mohamed Maroua. Though this group remained radical in their sermons, they were never violent until 2009 when they began to clash with government forces on account of disobedience to certain government orders. After one of their clashes in 2009 that left over 800 people dead, Mohammed Yusuf was arrested and detained by the police but he eventually died in custody under very controversial circumstances. A new leader, Abubakar Shekau emerged. He was a strong believer in the use of terrorism to advance the cause of this Boko Haram group. Abubakar Shekau was satanic and mindless. He acted like someone driven by demonic forces. He launched gruesome attacks on churches and mosques killing Christians and Muslims alike. It was a reign of terror in the north eastern part of Nigeria, kidnapping of women and school children, hostage taking and beheading of captives was common in the north east. His activities eventually plunged this group into an international network of terrorism that desires to establish an Islamic state within the borders of Nigeria, Cameroon, Chad and Niger Republic.

ACTIVITIES OF BOKO HARAM TERRORIST GROUP

Although Boko Haram was founded in 2002, their violent activities and reign of terror upon Nigeria citizens started effectively in 2009. This was following the announcement of Abubakar Shekau as the rightful successor of late Mohammed Yusuf[10]. Abubakar Shekau is a man with a pedigree for extreme radicalism and violence. He has severally been described as godless and satanic individual with a huge appetite for violence, destruction and bloodshed. In 2011, during the inauguration of President Goodluck Jonathan, Abubakar Shekau and his group organized the detonation of improvised Explosion Device near a military barrack in Bauchi State killing at least 10 innocent people. Precisely on 27 August 2011, the United Nations compound in Abuja was bombed killing about 18 persons and injuring may others. By November the same year, Boko Haram attacks have spread to Borno, Yobe and Adamawa states and making incursions into the territories of Cameroon, Chad and Niger Republic. In September 2013, several members of Boko

---

[10] Amy Mckenna, Boko Haram the Nigerian Islamic Group. https://www.britannica.com

Haram group dressed in Nigerian Army uniform formed a road check points during which they killed over 100 people. By 2014 Boko Haram was reported to have killed over 10,000 innocent men, women and children. One incident that shook Nigeria and the world was the kidnap of 276 school girls from Chibok in Borno state in April 2014. This happened barely a month after 51 students were massacred in their sleep at the Federal Government College Buni Yadi in Yobe state by this group.

It would be appropriate to say that 2014 remains the most gruesome year in the history of Boko Haram activities in Nigeria, this was the year they started using women and children including young girls for suicide bombing and beheading anyone who comes their way. In March 2015, Boko Haram pledged allegiance to the Islamic state of Iraq and Syria (ISIS).[11]

ISIS accepted the pledge and supported Boko Haram with training and ammunition while encouraging them to raise funds internally through kidnapping for ransom and attack on banks and other finance institutions. The support from ISIS was a tremendous boost to the activities of Boko Haram in the north eastern part of Nigeria, the boost was such that before the end of 2014, Boko Haram had absolute control of a number of local governments in the north east of Nigeria.

In August 2016 and in a bid to exercise more control over Boko Haram activities, ISIS appointed a new head for Boko Haram, Abu Musad-Al-Barnawi, who was meant to replace Abubakar

---

[11] Boko Haram purportedly pledges allegiance to ISIS, By Nima Elbagir, Paul Cruickshank and Mohammed Tawfeeq, CNN.

Shekau.[12] Following this appointment, Shekau released an audio message accusing Al-Barnawi of trying to stage a coup against him. He denounced ISIS declaration of Al-Barnawi as the new leader. Abubakar Shekau's extreme radicalism and his penchant to attack both Christians and Muslims and the use of children particularly young girls for suicide bombing brought him against the leadership of ISIS.

The rift between these 2 leaders grew progressively and eventually led to the creation of a splitter group called the Islamic State of West African Province (ISWAP). This group was led by Musad Al-Barnawi while Abubakar Shekau retained leadership of Boko Haram. Apparently, this split weakened the Boko Haram structure and contributed in easy recapture of all the Local Government areas that were under the control of Boko Haram.

Following counter offences launched by the Nigerian Armed Forces and the Multinational Joint Task Force, Boko Haram attacks were considerably reduced and they were pushed to the fringes of national borders. They now resort to attack on soft targets and ambush of military personnel. The Leader, Abubakar Shekau was reported to have been killed in one of the operations against the insurgents in August 2016. Though there was a video of a man who claimed to be Shekau in which he attempted to deny being killed. Indeed, the first report on the killing of Shekau came in 2009, shortly after he assumed leadership of the group, again he was reportedly killed during the battle of Kodunga in 2014. The Chadian President, Idris Deby also informed in mid-August 2015 that Shekau had been replaced by one Mohammed

---

[12] ISIS Proclaims 'New Leader' for Boko Haram, Conor Gafey, Nesweek 24 May 2020.

Daaud, while addressing reporters during the 55th independence anniversary celebration in Ndjamena.[13] However, in May 2021, the ISWAP released a tape in which they informed that Abubakar Shekau committed suicide by detonating a grenade on himself during an encounter with the group. The ISWAP leader, Abu Musab al-Barnawi, informed that his fighters captured Shekau and offered him a chance to repent and join his group but he preferred to commit suicide.

From the foregoing, there has been multiple reportage on the killing of Abubakar Shekau, it appears that the name Shekau is a pseudo name used by any member of the group who assumed position of leadership after the death of Abubakar Shekau. These tactics was also adopted by the Niger Delta militants when they used the name "Gbomo Jomo" to represent any one who assumes the positon of the spokesman for the group. This might be a strategy used by the insurgents to give an impression of invisibility and presence to their leadership.

---

[13] Sahara Reporters, New York, 12 August 2020.

GOVERNMENT ACTIONS AGAINST BOKO HARAM TERRORIST GROUP

Following the escalation of Boko Haram activities in the north eastern part of Nigeria in 2013, the Federal Government of Nigeria under President Good luck Jonathan ordered a major military offensive against the terrorist group. This was followed with declaration of state of emergency in Adamawa, Yobe and Borno states. As at this time, BHT had taken control of some of the local governments in these states. The sustained military operations mounted against the BHT group in 2014 did not yield any significant results. About 2 months to 2015 presidential election, Boko Haram was still in control of 13 local government areas in the North East. The situation came to a climax when it was barely one month to 2015 general election and the Boko Haram terrorist were still in control of some local government areas in the north eastern Nigeria. Consequently, presidential election was postponed for 2 weeks to enable a final onslaught on the locations of the insurgents. Yet only minimal achievements were made, just enough to enable the election take place. Despite the predominance of Boko Haram in certain local government areas in the north eastern Nigeria, human right organizations accused the Nigeria Armed Forces of high handedness, abuse of human rights and extrajudicial killings. This is akin to what is happening today in Cameroon, where Ambazonian fighters are beheading innocent civilians who they label "black legs" on allegation of sabotage while human right groups and some international organizations continue accusing the government of high handedness. In any case these accusations never deter the armed forces from carrying out their constitutional responsibilities.

The election of President Mohammed Buhari in 2015 marked a major turning point in the activities of the Insurgents in the north east of the country. In his inaugural speech, he ordered the relocation of the Military Command Centre for Operation Lafia Dole from Abuja to Maiduguri, the capital of Borno State. He made a major restructuring of the Armed Forces and appointed new Service Chiefs to head various arms of the Nigeria Armed Forces including the Police. The 7th Infantry Division that was established in 2013 to fight insurgency was reinvigorated with the introduction of new armament and other fighting platforms. A combat motorcycle unit was introduced as part of its 25th Task Force Brigade. Operation Lafia Dole was launched to replace Operation Zaman Lafia.

This was to fast track the counter insurgency operations and restore normalcy to the north east of Nigeria. It is important to recall that prior to the inauguration of Operation Lafia Dole, the entire north east of Nigeria was infested with the BHT. All these however began to change as troops of the operation in conjunction with the MNJTF launched a series of well-planned and well-coordinated joint ground and air operations. Operation

Rescue Final, Operation Rawa Kada, Operation Chikin Gudu and Operation Deep Punch were just some of the operations launched to root out the insurgents. The insurgents were flushed out of their tactical headquarter in Camp Zero in Sambisa forest during operation Deep Punch. To demonstrate this, the Chief of Army Staff celebrated 2017 Salah with troops in Sambisa forest and thereafter, he successfully conducted a gun firing exercise within the forest. All the local governments hitherto occupied by the insurgents were recovered and government presence established. The spiritual headquarter at Alargarno was also taken by the government troops. The insurgents were decimated to the extent that they lacked the capabilities to hold any territory in the north east of Nigeria. Though, the remnants of the insurgents took to their hills, they still are able to carry out occasional attacks on soft targets. Nevertheless, this group has remained technically defeated. It must be acknowledged that aggressive intelligence operations embarked upon by relevant agencies of Federal Government of Nigeria was highly instrumental to the weakening of the structure of the insurgents group which eventually culminated into a technical defeat, though some analysts have disputed this assertion, it will be discussed in subsequent section of this paper.

Generally speaking, there has been a deliberate and systematic restructure of the Nigeria Armed Forces to meet the changing demands of Counter Insurgency operation in Nigeria. For example, the Nigeria Navy created a Forward Operation Base in Baga fish dam. The Nigerian Air force upgraded its units in Maiduguri to a status of Division and established a Forward Operation Base in Monguno. There was a robust review of the Nigeria Army ground tactics including the introduction of the super camp concept. Some other actions of the government include:

(a) <u>Capacity Building Efforts.</u> The Nigerian armed forces have made numerous efforts to build capacity in response to contemporary security issues that challenge the corporate existence of the country. This has become very pertinent in view of the dynamic and broad nature of military operations. The armed forces can be engaged in a whole gamut of operations ranging from conventional wars and wars of asymmetric nature to complex and simple humanitarian operations, including peace support operations. Rear Admiral MM Kadiri, former Commandant, Nigerian National Defense College, in one of his addresses to the participants of Course 27 stated that defense management is a deep and complex subject, the more you get involved, the more you understand the complexities. This brings to fore, the need for continuous capacity building at all levels of the military for sustained operational effectiveness and service delivery. Capacity building is the strengthening of skills, competencies and abilities of people in order at which they are able to effectively work towards the achievement of organizational goals and objectives[14]. Consequent upon the need for a new capacity building, the armed forces have established

---

[14] Otu Offiong Duke "Capacity Building of the Nigeria Armed Forces and Security Challenges Published in International Journal of Trend in Scientific Research and Development(ijtsrd) ISSN2456 – 6470 Volume 4 December 2019 pp403.

a number of special forces training center; some of them are: The Nigerian Navy Special Boat Service (SBS) Ojo, the Nigerian Army Special Forces Schools (NASFS) at Buni Yadi, Yobe State, Counter Insurgency Center (CTCOIN) Jaji, Kaduna State and the Nigerian Army Training Center (NATRAC) Kontagora, Niger State. There is also a Special Force Command of the Nigerian Army with a command structure that coordinates the Special Force operations of the Nigerian Army. The Nigerian Army Peace Keeping Centre (NAPKC) that was created in 2009 to meet the peacekeeping requirements of African Union and ECOWAS, eventually expanded to include military courses approved by the United Nation Institute for Training and Research. Despite partnership with numerous nongovernmental organizations such as African Contingency Training and Assistance (ACTA), The German Technical Assistance Team (GTAT) and the British Training and Monitoring Team (BTMT), this institution has not paid adequate attention to asymmetric warfare training. This is because the current asymmetric situation was not envisaged at the time of setting up this institution. The Nigerian Air Force also has 3 special forces training schools in Kaduna, Bauchi and Osun State. Despite all these efforts, the number of persons' trained seem not to be enough to face the current challenges. It is therefore pertinent that deliberate efforts are made to establish more asymmetric warfare schools for the armed forces with a view to training larger number of personnel and impacting requisite skills. More could also be achieved if asymmetric warfare training is incorporated into the training curriculums of all the professional military training schools.

(b) <u>The Formation of Civilian Joint Task Force</u>. Volunteering members of the local population were organized into a civilian Joint Task Force. This was primarily to assist in the Intelligence gathering mechanism against the Boko Haram insurgents. This group have continued to play a fundamental role in the success of the operation.

(c) <u>Creation of a Command Information Sharing Grid</u>. A command information sharing grid was created for all the government agencies operating in the theatre for effective synergy of information. This remains a critical move and has been of tremendous help for the operations.

(d) <u>Creation of Super Camps</u>. This is a tactical change in the mode of operations that allows the use of large number of troops in engaging the enemy. The super camp concept adopted by the Nigeria Army has contributed in dealing a heavy blow on the insurgents and taking away initiative from them.

(e) <u>Introduction of a Legal Framework</u>. The Nigeria government introduced a comprehensive legal framework called the Terrorism Prevention Act of 2013. This was an amendment to the first counter terrorism act which was passed in 2011. The act sought to promote inter agency COIN efforts and also share responsibilities. The responsibility for coordinating all COIN efforts rests with the office of the National Security Adviser. In line with this Act, he is to, in conjunction with the Attorney

General of the Federation, ensure that all the counter insurgency efforts are in accordance with the international framework on counter terrorism.

(f) <u>Amnesty</u>. In attempt to peacefully resolve this crisis, Federal Government offered amnesty to this group which they rejected, and said that it was rather the Federal Government who deserves amnesty. Various attempt by the government to dialogue with this group has been scuttled by extreme radicalism and unwillingness of this group to toe the path of peace.

AN APPRAISAL OF COIN IN NIGERIA

For years it has proven difficult to determine the appropriate metrics to use in evaluating or assessing the success of operations against insurgents. However, a number of examples and a thorough appraisal of certain conditions of insurgency may help in arriving at an acceptable conclusion on the success or failure of counter insurgency operations generally.

David R Green, a former US Afghan war veteran, attempted to figure out the best measure for success in counter insurgency operations. He noted that it is inaccurate to use factors such as the number of insurgents killed, development projects completed and the number of meeting that the regular forces were able to hold with relevant authorities in determining the success of the operations. Also, Frank Ledwidge, in his book, Losing Small Wars: British Military Failure in Iraq and Afghanistan (Yale 2011) was of the opinion that there is no such thing as outright victory in counter insurgency[15]. He further opined that if the population is the price in counterinsurgency, then kinetic effects

---

[15] Frank Ledwidge, Losing Small Wars: British Military Failure in Iraq and Afghanistan, Yale 2011.

have no place in the campaign. Again, at the end of Russian invasion of Chechnya in 1999, the Russian government mentioned that the counterinsurgency operation in Chechnya was successful and that the insurgents have been largely crushed and relegated to occasional fringe attacks. Lorenzo Zambernardi an Italian academic, in his work "Counter insurgency Trilemma" maintained that counter insurgency involve 3 main goals and that a counter insurgent can only achieve 2 of these goals. He identified the Impossible Trilemma of counter insurgency as:

(a) Force Protection.
(b) Distinguishing between combatants and non-combatants.
(c) Physical elimination of the insurgents.

He noted that a state can protect its force while destroying the insurgents but only by indiscriminately killing the civilians. Protecting civilians and own force means abandoning the objective of physically destroying the insurgents. Finally, a state can distinguish between combatants and noncombatants while killing the insurgents but at the increased risk of its own troops.

In the case of Boko Haram insurgents, it must be noted that the strategic end state for this group was to create an Islamic State in the Sahel, covering part of Nigeria, Cameroon, Chad and Niger. Despite the support from ISIS, this desire has not been achieved. Earlier efforts to evaluate the success of COIN operations against the Boko Haram insurgents has been controversial owing to the complex nature of asymmetric warfare. Nevertheless, it was aptly captured by Colonel Timothy Antiagha of the Nigeria Army in his article, "State of Counter Insurgency Operations". He noted that fixation on the assessment metrics developed for conventional wars hampers a clear and objective evaluation or assessment of success of the Boko Haram counter insurgency operation. Like he rightly observed, metrics evaluation is largely irrelevant to the situation at hand and accounts for the inaccurate and misleading conclusions on the success of Boko Haram counter insurgency operations. Some critical factors that can be used to determine the success of counter insurgency operation including those already identified by Colonel Antiagha in his article are as follows:

(a) <u>Inability of the Insurgents to Reach their Strategic end State.</u> The strategic end state of the Boko Haram terrorist was to establish an Islamic state in the area covering north east Nigeria, northern part of Cameroon, part of Chad and Niger Republic. As at today, nothing of such exists in these areas. All these areas still remain under the authority of their respective government.

(b) <u>The Freedom Which a Nations Security Forces Enjoy in the Conduct of Military Operations</u>. Before the arrival of the President Mohammed Buhari in 2015, Boko Haram terrorist were in control of about 13 Local government areas in the north east of Nigeria. They had their flags hoisted and collected tax from locals within these territories. Today all the Local government areas and towns under the control of Boko Haram have been liberated.

(c) <u>Exercise of Political Authority</u>: The exercises of political authority is a key factors in determining the success of military operation in an asymmetric environment. Despite the desire of this group to establish an Islamic state in the north east of Nigeria, they do not exercise any form of political or administrative control in the place. The Federal government of Nigeria currently exercises political and administration control over all parts of north east. Thanks to the counter insurgency efforts of the government.

(d) <u>Legal Indicators</u>: Certain legal indicators such as law making, law enforcement and prosecution of offenders may be relevant in assessing who is in control of a particular area in contest. In the north eastern state of Nigeria, the state remains the only institution that make the law, enforces and prosecute offenders including captured members of Boko Haram terrorists group.

(e) <u>Population Support</u>: The support from the local population is also fundamental in gauging the success of the counter insurgent operation. The willingness of the local population to provide intelligence and the activities of the civilian JTF speaks volume on the amount of support the operations gets from the population in the north east. The civilian population form the hub of the intelligence gathering process in the counter insurgency operation against BHT.

(f) <u>Freedom to Bear Fire Arms.</u> Only members of the Nigerian security forces can exercise the freedom to bear arms openly in the north east and indeed in any other part of Nigeria. Any other individuals or group that bear fire arms does that clandestinely and run a risk of of being arrested and prosecuted by the members of the security forces.

(g) <u>Control of Communication and Transport</u>: The control of the communication network and transport system in the environment of asymmetry is critical in determining the success of counter insurgency operations. All the roads that were formally closed for safety reasons have been opened for commuters.

(h) <u>Number of Surrendered Insurgents</u>: A good number of Boko Haram fighters have surrendered their weapons and presented themselves for demobilization and deradicalization within the framework of Operation Safe Corridor. On the 19 August 2020, troops of the MNJTF in N'Djamena received 106 former Boko Haram fighters who surrendered. This is an indication that this group has been degraded and are on the last phase of their existence.

(i) Authority Receiving Surrendering Combatants: Following the death of Shekau and continued bombardment of Boko Haram location, thousands of their fighters and their families are repenting and surrendering to the Nigeria Aremed Forces. Over 4000 fighters have surrendered from May 2021 to November 2021.

The occasional attacks and suicide bombing experienced in the part of the country is simply a sign of a weakening insurgency. Such actions are primarily to compensate their sponsors and give feeling of presence even though they have failed and lost hope on the possibility of achieving their end state. In view of this forgoing, the assertion by the Nigeria government that Boko Haram has been technically defeated is valid.

THE LAKE CHAT OPTION

Lake Chad is a fresh water lake located within the Chad basin. It is the biggest lake in the Sahel zone on West and Central Africa. It is one of the largest lakes in Africa with its surface area varying from season to season and from year to year. The smallest area was recorded in 1986 at 279 Square Kilometer.[16] However, recent reports have indicated an improvement from this level. The River Chari Logone in the Republic of Chad supplies 90 percent of the water in the Lake. River Yobe in Nigeria also supplies a littlie amount of water to the Lake. The lake is dotted by numerous small islands and area of swampland across the middle dividing the northern and southern halves of the Lake. It is generally shallow with a maximum depth of about 10.5 meters and this accounts for its seasonal change is size. The surface area of the lake as at 2020 is about 1,540 Kilometer Square with an average depth of 1.5 meters.[17] This lake is economically important as it provides arable land for agriculture and water for over 30 million people living around the lake. Expectedly, fishing and

---

[16] Umar, IA, (2018): Modelling of water cycle regime of Lake Chad using GIS and rmote sensing for decadal periods.
[17] Odada, Oyebande and Oguntola 2020.

agriculture form the primary activity for the sustenance of the population of the the Lake Chad basin. This basin has an area of about 2.4 square kilometers comprising of 8 countries but only 4 of them have direct contact with the Lake.[18] The countries are Nigeria, Cameroon, Chad and Niger Republic. Incidentally, these countries have remained among the poorest and most unstable countries in the world despite the opportunities that this natural endowment could offer.

EFFECT OF CLIMATE CHANGE ON LAKE CHAD

Due to climate change coupled with increasing human activities, the Lake Chat basin has suffered the largest documented destruction of biodiversity globally. In the last thirty years, water demand for irrigation has remarkably increased thereby increasing the pressure on the water available in the Lake. For instance, between 1983 and 1994, irrigation demand has grown by 200%, leading to water resource overexploitation.[19] Twenty years earlier, in 1963, Lake Chad covered an area of over 20,000 square kilometers but has shrunk by over 90 per cent of its size primarily as a result of climate change. At the same time, the local population is growing with a rapidly degreasing surface water. More islands began to appear in spaces that where hitherto occupied by water thereby attracting new fishing settlements.

---

[18] Global Water Patnership(GWP), Lake Chad factsheet(Oct 2013)
[19] Ibid

IMPACT ON THE POPULATION

The combine effect of climate change, decreased precipitation, drought and other human activities have negatively affected the volume of water in the Lake Chad. This lake is reported to have lost over 90 per cent of it's volume as at 1963 and this has a consequential effect on over 30 million people who depend on this lake for survival[20]. The consequences of this disappearance of Lake Chad ranges from economic hardship to insecurity thereby denying the people from benefiting from the basic essence of governance. A fresh water lake that supports fishing, agriculture, irrigation, domestic use and other economic activity both in Chad, Cameroon, Nigeria and Niger Republic disappearing with a period of 50 years is bound to force the people to search for other means of survival. The fight for a dwindling resources in the face of a rapidly increasing human population becomes real. This is a clear compliance with the theory of Thomas Malthus, an 18th century British philosopher and economist known for the Malthusian growth model. The theory states that food production will not be able to keep up with growth in the human population resulting in disease, famine, war and calamity.[21] This calamity has eventually befallen the people of the Lake Chad region largely on account of the activities of the Boko Haram terrorist group. It is strongly believed that terrorist activities and general insecurity in this region is largely exacerbated by the disappearance of Lake Chad with and attendant scarcity of resources.

As the Lake gradually disappears, most men in the

---

[20] www.climate-change-guide.com/effects-of-climate-change.html.

[21] https://www.investopemedia.com

communities begin to seek for greener pasture elsewhere, some move to the big cities in dry season when the Lake can no longer sustain them. Therefore, Internal migration is increasing, as well as people embarking on dangerous missions through the Sahel and the Mediterranean Sea to places in Europe for better life. The women and children left behind have to fill the gaps and are forced to innovate to maintain food security. The people of this region constitute the poorest in the world and they live in the most unstable political and economic environment.

IMPACT ON THE SECURITY OF THE REGION

The dramatic disappearance of Lake Chad has had devastating impacts on Nigeria.[22] Consequently, this Lake has been severely labeled an ecological catastrophe by the United Nations. Human population expansion and unsustainable human water extraction from Lake Chad have caused several natural species to be stressed and threatened by declining lake levels

The shrinking of the lake has been at the base of several conflicts that broke out in this region over the years. The population have defied national borders as the communities recede along with the Lake irrespective of the national boundaries. Countries bordering Lake Chad argue over the rights to the remaining areas of water. Along with international conflicts, violence between countries is also increasing among the lake's dwellers. Farmers and herders want the water for their crops and livestock and are constantly diverting the water while the lake's fishermen want

---

[22] Damilola Oyedele (11 May 2017). "The dwindling lake". *D+C, development and cooperation*. Retrieved 14 June 2017.

water diversion slowed or halted in order to prevent continuing decline in water levels resulting in further strain on the lake's fish.[23] Furthermore, populations of birds and other animals in the area are threatened, including those that serve as important sources of food for the local human population.

WAY FORWARD

Returning the water back into the Lake Chad would be an effective counter insurgency measure that would ultimately address the question of insecurity in Nigeria and other countries within the Chad basin. The disappearance of this vast body of water in the North-East of Nigeria has not only constituted a major source of headache for the communities within the basin but for the United Nations and other international organizations with great concern for the survival of humanity. This concern was deservedly raised by the President of the United Nations General Assembly, Maria Espinosa-Garces, during her visit to Nigeria. She aptly described what is left of the great lake as one of Africa's major climate change disasters.

This is inline with earlier description of the crisis by the United Nation as an ecological disaster of monumental proportion. A large expanse of water that covered 25,000 square kilometers in the 1960s is now reduced to a small lake of just about about 2,500 km2, while the depth that measured up to 11 meters is now reduced to an average of 1.2 meters. Also disappearing with the water is the diverse community of wild animals, birds, fish and

---

[23] "Case study on river management: Lake Chad".13 February 2018.

plants.[24] The Nigerian Foreign Affairs Minister, Mr Geoffrey Onyema described this as an existential issue, for a lake that supports over 30 million inhabitants to loose over 90 per cent of its volume; he added that map of Nigeria without a depiction of Lake Chad, as is customary, will soon become a reality.

The denial of a means of livelihood is largely believed to be at the root of the escalation of insecurity especially terrorism, banditry and other forms of violent extremism, in the North-East of the country and beyond. Survival is a natural instinct of every human being, hence deprived of their grazing land by desertification, arms-bearing Fulani herdsmen have taken to invading people's farmland, even in the most southerly states, and unleashing terror on whoever dares to stand in their way. The farmers and fishermen, having lost their hitherto fertile land and water to the rapidly encroaching desert dunes, have either taken to new trade or moved to other parts of the country in search of greener pastures. A large number of these farmers feel threated by the presence of these migrants and immigrants searching for greener pasture, hence they have also picked up arms to defend themselves against invading headers. This is all in a deliberate struggle for survival, which is a normal and acceptable human phenomenon.

In the midst of this struggle, a lot of able bodied young men and women are left without jobs or any form of vocation, they are vulnerable and easy recruit in the hands of Boko Haram. The ideology of Boko Haram can easily be sold to a man who is desperate for survival and they find a lot of comfort within the ranks of the jihadists.

---

[24] Taiwa Ojoye, Punch Newspaper, 15 May 2019.

In 2009, the United Nations Food and Agriculture Organization warned of the consequences of the disappearance of Lake Chad 20 years' time, calling for a radical change in water management techniques. "The humanitarian disaster that could follow the ecological catastrophe needs urgent interventions," FAO's Director of Land and Water Division, Parvjs Koohafkan, said then.[25] Consequently, the Lake Chad Basin Commission has organized a series of events to create awareness on the need to save Lake Chad. The option of recharging the Lake by creating a waterway all the way from River Congo was critically consider as a viable option to save the Lake. This is more so as some of the rivers that fed the lake, namely Chari-Logone, Hadejia, Yobe, Jama'are, Yedseram and Ngadda, has been disrupted by careless and indiscriminate construction of dams and abstraction of water for irrigation.[26]

Recharging the lake from fresh sources of water remains the only viable solution, as climate change has largely disrupted the rainfall patter that has taken its toll on the Lake. In this regard, a scheme to channel water from the Congo River, through Chari River to Lake Chad is still relevant today as it was in 1982 when it was first mooted. There was another plan to divert water from River Ubangi, a tributary of River Congo, into the Lake through the same Chari in the Central African Republic. The result of a feasibility study shows that this project is achievable though it would cost as much as 50 billion United States dollars. This option, despite its viability has not seen the light of the day either as a result of the huge amount of money required for the project

---

[25] Ibid

[26] Taiwa Ojoye, Punch Newspaper, 15 May 2019.

or unwillingness of the United Nations and other concerned members of the international community to adopt this option. The cost of this project might be quite huge but it is nothing compared to what is spent managing the crisis created by the disappearance of the Lake.

Cases of man-made water channels and beaches abound that should serve as an incentive for the Chad project. The Suez Canal in Egypt, for instance, one of the most heavily used shipping lanes linking the Mediterranean in the north to in the Red Sea in the south, shows that the Lake Chad project is achievable. Besides, in Barcelona, an artificial beach was created to give the city that hosted the 1992 Olympic Games a facelift. Dubai also offers a good example of where water is taken from the sea to make life habitable in a desert. If these can be done, it is also possible to channel water into the Lake in order to restore its lost glory. Doing so may not solve all the problems of Nigeria's North-East, but will go a long way in ameliorating them.

CONCLUSION

Post independent counter insurgency operations in Nigeria dates back to 1966 following the declaration of the Niger Delta Republic by Major Isaac Adaka Boro. This insurgency was quickly brought to an end by armed forces of Nigeria within 12 days of its commencement. This was again followed by the declaration of the Republic of Biafra in 1967 by Colonel Chukwuemeka Odumegwu Ojukwu. This eventually degenerated into a full blown war that lasted for 3 years with capitulation of the Biafra troop before the Nigeria Armed Forces. Despite crushing these 2 major insurgent groups over 50 years ago by the Nigerian Armed Forces, their vestiges still linger in certain parts of Nigeria. This is evident in the activities of the IPOB in south east of Nigeria and various Niger Delta liberation movement in the south south region of Nigeria, coupled with the activities of the BHT in the north east of Nigeria.

The election of President Mohammed Buhari marked a turning point in the activities of the Boko Haram group in the north east of Nigeria. President Buhari quickly effected some structural changes in the Armed Forces including the relocation of the Military Command Centre for Operation Lafia Dole from Abuja to Maiduguri, the theatre of operation. Gradually and consistently the armed forces of Nigeria launched a number of operations that drove out these insurgents from all their strong holds in the north east. Today, the BHT are not in control of any local government nor any territories within the Federal Republic of Nigeria. The Nigeria government has announced a technical defeat of this group. This group now resort to suicide bombing and occasional attacks on soft targets, nevertheless this does not invalidate the fact that they are technically defeated.

One of the most fundamental efforts of the government in the fight against insurgency is centered on capacity building. The Nigerian Army, Navy and the Air Force established a number of Special Forces training schools and further went into partnership with some nongovernmental organizations to enhance the capacity of the armed forces personnel in the fight against insurgents. However there still remain a good number of personnel who have not received comprehensive training on asymmetric warfare, hence a training gap exists within the ranks of our personnel. There is therefore the need to systematically increase the number of personnel with asymmetric warfare training through the establishment of more schools and incorporating the training into the curriculum of all military training institutions in the country.

The government of the Federal Republic of Nigeria has taken a number of measures to counter insurgency in Nigeria however, there hasn't been adequate attention paid to the Lake Chad option.

A non kinetic option that could dramatically return peace to most part of Nigeria and other areas within the Lake Chad basin. This is largely because, at the root of the crisis, lies poverty, hunger and deprivation of means of livelihood. Returning the Lake Chad back to 90 percent of its original volume may have the potentials of reducing the crisis tremendously.

RECOMMENDATIONS

It is recommended that:

a. The capacity for counter insurgency should be enhanced through the incorporation of asymmetric warfare training in all military training institutions while establishing more schools that would be purely dedicated to asymmetric warfare training.

b. The the Lake Chad Basin Commission prioritizes the recharging of Lake Chad project and see that it is realized with the support of the United Nations.

Printed in the United States
by Baker & Taylor Publisher Services